Fighting Infectious Disease

Sally Morgan

Heinemann
LIBRARY

www.heinemann.co.uk/library
Visit our website to find out more information about **Heinemann Library** books.

To order:
☎ Phone 44 (0) 1865 888066
🖹 Send a fax to 44 (0) 1865 314091
🖳 Visit the Heinemann Bookshop at www.heinemann.co.uk/library to browse our catalogue and order online.

First published in Great Britain by Heinemann Library, Halley Court, Jordan Hill, Oxford OX2 8EJ, a division of Reed Educational and Professional Publishing Ltd. Heinemann is a registered trademark of Reed Educational and Professional Publishing Ltd.

OXFORD MELBOURNE AUCKLAND JOHANNESBURG BLANTYRE
GABORONE IBADAN PORTSMOUTH NH (USA) CHICAGO

Designed by Tinstar Design (www.tinstar.co.uk)
Illustrations by Art Construction
Originated by Ambassador Litho Ltd.
Printed and bound in Hong Kong/China

ISBN 0 431 14884 8
06 05 04 03 02
10 9 8 7 6 5 4 3 2 1

British Library Cataloguing in Publication Data
Morgan, Sally
       Fighting infectious disease. – (Science at the edge)
       1.Immunology – Juvenile literature
       I.Title
       616'.079

Acknowledgements
The Publisher would like to thank the following for permission to reproduce photographs: AKG: p4; Bruce Coleman Collection: p15; Corbis: p43; Ecoscene: p53; FLPA: p32; Image Select/WHO: p7; Environmental Images: John Booth p52; Format: Michael Ann Mullen p50; Panos Pictures: p28; Planet Earth Pictures: p47; Popperfoto: p22; Popperfoto/Reuters: pp5, 41, 49; Science Photo Library: pp9, 10, 11, 13, 14, 17, 18, 19, 23, 25, 26, 30, 34, 36, 38, 39, 42, 45, 55, 57.

Cover photograph reproduced with permission of Popperfoto.

Our thanks to Dr Michael Winson for his assistance in the preparation of this book.

Every effort has been made to contact copyright holders of any material reproduced in this book. Any omissions will be rectified in subsequent printings if notice is given to the Publisher.

Any words appearing in the text in bold, **like this**, are explained in the Glossary.

Contents

Introduction

During the Middle Ages, bubonic plague, or Black Death, as it was commonly known, swept across Europe. It was named after the dark bruises that appeared on the skin of its victims. It killed quickly, with people dying within days of the appearance of swellings in the armpits and groin – and there was no cure. Between 1347 and 1350, one in every three people died from this horrible disease and the death toll probably exceeded 25 million. When we read about the Black Death, we probably think that this could never happen today. But it does. While millions have been saved by modern medicine, the death toll worldwide each year from preventable and curable diseases is 11 million. There is much more work to be done.

Bubonic plague killed many millions during the Middle Ages. It is a disease which still kills many thousands of people today.

'Many dropped dead in the open streets, both by day and by night, whilst a great many others, though dying in their own houses, drew their neighbours' attention to the fact more by the smell of their rotting corpses than by any other means.'
The Black Death, as recorded by Giovanni Boccaccio, who lived in Florence, Italy

What is a disease?

A disease is a condition that arises when something goes wrong with the normal working of the body. As a result we become ill. The signs of a disease can include things everyone might recognize – headache, fever, sore throat and rashes on the body. These are called symptoms, and they help a doctor to diagnose or identify the disease and decide how to treat it.

An **infectious** disease is one which can be passed from one person to another. These diseases are caused by micro-organisms such as bacteria and viruses that are in the air we breathe, the water we use for drinking and washing, and in the soil. Fortunately, the human body is well equipped with natural barriers and an **immune system** to fight off these organisms. Unfortunately, natural barriers can fail and then we become infected.

This book looks at some of the infectious diseases that affect humans and the organisms that cause them. Some of the diseases that you will read about in this book have infected humans for thousands of years, these include major killers such as **smallpox** and influenza (**flu**). The book also looks at some of the emerging and re-emerging diseases that have appeared in recent years, such as **HIV-AIDS**, **tuberculosis** (TB), **Ebola** and **hantavirus**, and looks at questions such as 'how do bacteria become **resistant** to drugs?', 'how can we fight tuberculosis?' and 'will we ever live in a disease-free world?'

Protective clothing is essential when dealing with deadly infectious diseases such as Congo fever and Ebola. This senior nursing sister is collecting blood samples which have been taken from patients suffering from Congo fever.

Modern medicine

Today's young people are very fortunate. They are the first generation ever to have the means of protecting themselves from the most deadly and common **infectious** diseases. Many of them can go to doctors who help prevent or cure diseases such as **malaria**, **tuberculosis** (TB), **pneumonia** and **measles**. Just 150 years ago, four out of every ten people died prematurely from an infectious disease. The **smallpox** virus killed millions, but it is now extinct, although there are some frozen stocks in research institutes. Major killers such as **whooping cough**, **polio** and scarlet fever (named after the bright red rash it causes) have been, or are on the verge of being, controlled.

Developed vs developing world

Everybody can contract a disease, regardless of their race, gender or wealth. However, their survival rate and the quality of medical care that they receive depends on where they live. The developed parts of the world such as Europe, North America and Australasia have high standards of living and hygiene, and good quality medical facilities. Most children are **vaccinated** against childhood diseases. In addition, children receive good health education at school. As a result, the number of people suffering from infectious diseases has fallen dramatically and life expectancy is increasing.

But the story is very different in the developing world such as parts of Africa, South America and Asia. Infectious diseases are responsible for almost half of all deaths and they are the leading killer of young people under 20. These deaths occur primarily among the poorest people because they do not have access to the drugs and facilities necessary for prevention or cure. Approximately half of the deaths from infectious disease are caused by just three diseases – malaria, TB and **HIV** infection (which leads to **AIDS**). These three diseases cause more than 300 million illnesses and 5 million deaths each year. Malaria is a big killer. It is caused by a tiny single-celled organism that infects red blood cells, and it is carried by the female mosquito. Every year more than 300 million people are infected and at least 1 million are killed. In fact, one child dies of malaria every 40 seconds. These deaths are unnecessary, as many of the diseases could be prevented or treated with equipment and medicines that often cost less than £1.

Over the last few decades there has been a considerable advance in the treatment of diseases. There are three main approaches:

1 Prevention in the form of improved standards of hygiene and a better understanding of how disease-causing organisms are spread.
2 Prevention by vaccinating to protect the body against disease.
3 Using drugs, such as **antibiotics**, to kill the disease-causing organisms that have infected the body.

'It's like loading up seven Boeing 747 airliners each day and crashing them into Mount Kilimanjaro.'

Dr W. Kilama, Chairman of Malaria Foundation International, talking about the number of people dying from malaria

World Health Organization

The World Health Organization (WHO) was founded in 1948 as an agency of the United Nations. It provides information on health issues and sets global standards for health. It also works with governments to develop national health programmes. The WHO is a key player in making essential drugs available to people who cannot afford them, creating healthier cities and promoting healthy lifestyles and environments. Its most successful campaign, started in 1967, completely **eradicated** smallpox by 1980. It involved a programme of vaccination in countries where smallpox was **endemic**. A number of other diseases targeted by the WHO are on the brink of eradication, including polio and **leprosy**. However, as some diseases are eradicated, others appear – so the work of the WHO never ends.

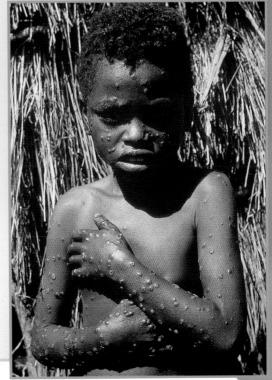

This child is at the latter stage of smallpox, when the body is covered by fluid-filled pustules. These dry up and form scabs that are filled with viral particles, which can be spread by contact.

What causes disease?

Bacteria and viruses can infect other organisms and cause disease. They are described as being pathogenic, which means 'to give rise to suffering'. Highly virulent bacteria or viruses are those that infect other organisms very easily and spread quickly, for example **typhoid** bacteria. In contrast, some of the bacteria responsible for food poisoning and **leprosy** have low virulence.

Disease-causing bacteria can be carried by people who do not show any symptoms of the disease. However, these people (called carriers) can spread the bacteria so other people become infected. Typhoid, for example, can be caught from a carrier. Carriers working in places such as kitchens can infect tens, even hundreds of people.

Disease-causing organisms enter our bodies through **membranes** in the mouth or nose, or through cuts or open wounds in the skin. Once inside the body they multiply rapidly. It may be some time before the individual feels ill. This length of time is called the incubation period. It varies from a few days to several weeks, even months.

The majority of disease-causing organisms are bacteria and viruses, but **fungi**, **protozoa** and flat worms can cause disease too.

Bacteria

Bacteria are found everywhere – in the soil, water or air, in cold and hot places. A typical bacterium is about a thousandth of a millimetre in length. Different species of bacteria have different cell shapes. Spherical bacteria, called cocci, can occur as single cells or in pairs. Streptococci, which cause sore throats, group together in long chains. There are also rod-shaped bacteria such as the ones that cause typhoid, those that have a bent rod shape such as **cholera** bacteria, and spiral-shaped ones that cause **syphilis**.

Bacteria can reproduce asexually (without requiring another organism) by simply dividing into two. Under favourable conditions, where there is plenty of food, bacteria can divide every 20 minutes or so. This means that overnight one bacterium could have multiplied to more than eight and a half million in number.

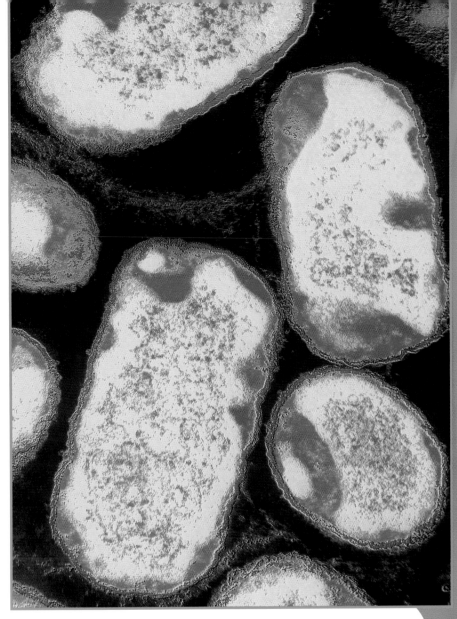

A bacterium has a cell structure that is much simpler than a human cell. There is a cell wall and a cell membrane. Inside is a length of **DNA**, the genetic material.

How do they work?
Once inside the body, bacteria attack its cells. Some stick to the outside of cells by means of threads called pili, which harm the cells. Others produce **toxins**. Some toxins, called exotoxins, are released by living bacteria. Others, called endotoxins, are released when the bacterium dies and its cell contents spill out. Endotoxins cause food poisoning.

Viruses

Viruses are the smallest known organisms. A typical virus is just 100 nanometres wide (one nanometre is one millionth of a millimetre). They are very unusual organisms as they do not have a cell membrane or any cell components, and they can only reproduce inside a living cell. The rest of the time, when they are outside of a living organism, they are inactive. Some viruses can survive for years outside of a cell, but others can only survive a few hours. Viral diseases are probably the most important group of diseases. They pose problems as there are few treatments for them and they are unaffected by **antibiotics**. Therefore, viral diseases have to be prevented rather than cured.

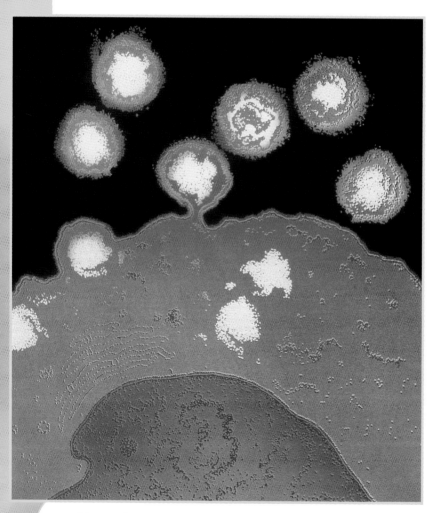

The small spheres are human immunodeficiency viruses (**HIV**), which are being released from an infected human cell. Each virus has the potential to infect another cell.

Viral infections

Viruses infect cells by attaching to the cell surface. Then they inject a length of **nucleic acid** into the cell. This takes over the cell, instructing it to make copies of the virus. This takes about 30–60 minutes, after which time the cell bursts and thousands of copies of the virus are released. The new copies infect other cells and so the cycle continues with the numbers of infected cells increasing. Each virus has its own preferred type of cell to infect. This is called the host cell.

1 The virus approaches a cell.

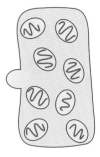

4 New viruses are formed within the cell.

2 The virus sticks to the cell **membrane** and injects its nucleic acid into the cell.

3 The nucleic acid multiplies inside the cell.

5 The cell bursts and the new viruses are released.

Parasites

Parasitic diseases are caused by one organism living in and feeding off another, called the host. Although the **parasite** may weaken the host, it does not usually kill it immediately. Parasitic infections often weaken the body's defence system through blood-loss, malnutrition, tissue and organ damage. Infected individuals may die from kidney or liver failure and the presence of the parasite in their body makes them more susceptible to other diseases.

A large number of people suffer from parasitic diseases. The diseases are difficult to control because of the ways in which the parasites spread. Major parasitic diseases include **malaria**, sleeping sickness (a disease carried by the tsetse fly in Africa) and amoebic dysentery (caused by a protozoan). Bilharzia (also called schistosomiasis) is caused by a blood fluke – a type of flat worm. The eggs of the fluke can block small blood vessels in the brain and spinal cord. People become infected by bathing in or drinking water infected with the blood fluke larvae. Today this disease infects more than 200 million people in developing countries. There are a few parasitic fungi, which cause skin diseases such as athlete's foot and ringworm.

The tapeworm lives in animal intestines, where it absorbs food. The worm's 'head' bears suckers and hooks that attach it to the intestinal wall. The worm produces lots of eggs, which are passed out with the animal's **faeces** and may be picked up by another animal, which then becomes infected with larval worms.

Malaria

The most important parasitic disease is malaria. It is caused by a tiny parasite that is carried from person to person by the female anopheles mosquito. When the mosquito bites through a person's skin, it injects a tiny drop of saliva into the blood to stop the blood from clotting. Any parasites in its saliva get into the blood stream at the same time. And, if a female mosquito bites an infected person, it sucks up the infected blood into its stomach. Hence the mosquito is a vector, or carrier, of the disease. The malaria parasites invade the red blood cells, where they grow and multiply. The cells then burst open, releasing many parasites which infect more cells.

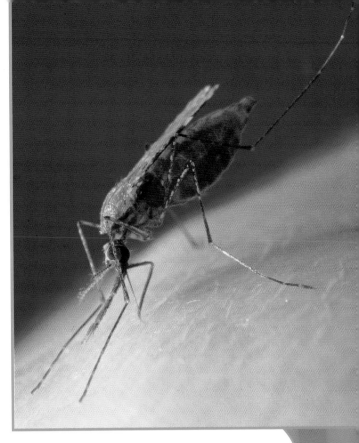

A female anopheles mosquito uses her sharp mouth parts to pierce through the skin to reach blood vessels.

Malaria is a serious disease that causes bouts of fever, sweating and shivering. However, it can be treated with drugs. In order to prevent the possibility of catching the disease, people visiting countries where malaria is present take anti-malarial drugs that stop the parasites surviving in their bodies. They can also take measures to avoid being bitten by the mosquitoes. For example, by using mosquito repellents and covering their arms and legs at dusk when the mosquitoes are most active.

'My husband works as a logger in the jungle. He's gone for weeks at a time and he gets malaria. It's a terrible thing to have. Sweating. Very bad headaches. High, high fever. You vomit. You are so weak. When malaria comes every few days, you feel like you want to die.'
Sujatin, resident of Irian Jaya, Indonesia (quoted from *Malaria Smithsonian Magazine*)

Spreading disease

Disease-causing organisms are spread in many different ways, depending on the parts of the body that they infect and whether they can survive for long outside of the body. The most common ways are via droplets in the air (nasal or mouth secretions), food and water, direct contact or by animals.

When you cough or sneeze, thousands of tiny droplets shoot out into the air. If you have the common cold or **flu**, the virus contained in the droplets will spread rapidly to other people — especially in crowded places, such as trains and buses.

Carried in food and water

Several diseases are carried into the body with food and drink, for example **typhoid** and **cholera**. Water is usually treated to kill any bacteria and viruses, making it safe to drink. However, in some places, water treatment is inadequate and the water may be contaminated with sewage (waste matter).

Food can also contain bacteria if it is prepared in conditions of poor hygiene. Because the **faeces** of a person suffering from a bacterial disease, such as typhoid or cholera, may contain the bacteria, it is vitally important that people wash their hands after visiting the toilet and before handling food. The eggs of tapeworms and other intestinal **parasites** can also pass out with the faeces of infected people. These diseases spread if the faeces contaminate food or drinking water. This means that they are common after flooding or other major disasters, when sewage systems are disrupted and the drinking water is contaminated.

If food is insufficiently cooked, it may also contain harmful bacteria. All the bacteria will be killed if it is cooked at a high temperature.

Salmonella bacteria

The term 'food poisoning' is used to describe an infection of the gut following the eating of infected food or water. Two types of food poisoning – Salmonella and typhoid – are caused by related *Salmonella* bacteria. *Salmonella typhi*, which causes typhoid, spreads in water supplies that are contaminated by human faeces and it can also be found on food that is under-cooked. The bacteria cause severe inflammation of the small intestine, diarrhoea, high fever and slow heart rate. **Antibiotics** are given to treat the infection. Salmonella food poisoning can be contracted by eating meat, milk, eggs and chicken that are contaminated with *Salmonella enteritidis*. The bacteria are digested in the intestine, causing the release of an endotoxin (see page 9), which leads to the symptoms of food poisoning – fever, diarrhoea and vomiting. Until recently, infection with *Salmonella enteritidus* was the most common cause of food poisoning, but this has been overtaken by bacteria such as *Listeria* and *Campylobacter*.

Many diseases are spread by animals. Cockroaches (shown here) and flies pick up bacteria and viruses and then spread them as they walk over food surfaces. Rats often live in sewers where they pick up bacteria. They spread the bacteria when they come above ground and run around kitchens.

Keeping clean

Disinfectants, antiseptics and **sterilization** have an important role to play in controlling the spread of disease.

Our skin is covered with micro-organisms. We continually handle objects that have been touched by other people or animals, and the micro-organisms may come into contact with our mouth (on food) or other parts of our body. In order to keep the skin clean and free of harmful bacteria we need to wash with soap. Cleaning your hands after visiting the toilet is particularly important in order to prevent the transmission of disease-causing bacteria and viruses. People involved with food preparation have to maintain strict standards of hygiene to prevent food becoming contaminated with disease-causing bacteria.

Disinfectants (made from chemicals) are used to kill bacteria and viruses that lurk in kitchens and bathrooms. Nowadays, it is possible to buy kitchen cloths, chopping boards, soaps, washing-up liquids and so on which have been impregnated with antibacterial agents. However, bacteria are found in the air and on every surface, so it is impossible to make a room such as a kitchen 'germ-free'.

Dirt is good for you

Nowadays we can wipe surfaces with antibacterial cloths, shower with antibacterial soap, and sleep beneath an antibacterial quilt. But scientists are now finding evidence that our lack of contact with dirt and bacteria may be the cause of the rapid rise in asthma, hay fever and diabetes. During the first few years of life, the body is exposed to all sorts of micro-organisms and this stimulates the **immune system**. In today's hygiene-obsessed world, children have less contact with dirt. Children are also **vaccinated** to protect them from childhood diseases, but exposure to these diseases is now thought to protect the body from allergies. This would suggest that getting dirty when you are young can be good for you!

Sterile operating theatres

A wound or cut can easily become **septic**. This can be prevented by cleaning the wound with an antiseptic that will kill the harmful bacteria. There are some places, however, where it is even more important to prevent bacterial contamination, for example hospital operating theatres. The opening up of the body during surgery can leave it exposed to possible bacterial infection. Therefore, all of the equipment and clothing used in an operating theatre has to be sterilized using an autoclave. This destroys all bacteria, **fungi** and viruses. An autoclave is similar to a pressure cooker. When pressure is applied to a sealed container of water, the water boils at a higher temperature and this is enough to kill all micro-organisms. Often it is impossible to ensure that the equipment is sterilized, so disposable equipment is used. Disposable equipment is prepared in 'clean room conditions', packaged and then irradiated (treated with electromagnetic radiation) to kill all the micro-organisms. Immediately after a piece of equipment is removed from its sterilized packaging, it is used once and then thrown away.

Blood screening

Many diseases are carried in the blood, so there is a risk that people will contract a disease when they are given a blood transfusion. Tests are carried out on every unit of donated blood to make sure it is safe to use. The tests are specific to a particular disease, and sensitive enough to detect tiny amounts of bacteria, viruses or **antibodies** to the **infectious** agent in a blood sample. It is normal to test for **HIV**, **hepatitis** B and **syphilis**, but some countries require tests for hepatitis C, Chagas' disease (a type of sleeping-sickness disease) and **malaria**. Tests that can detect the tiniest amounts of bacterial or viral **DNA** in the blood sample are now being developed. They will enable doctors to reject blood that contains previously undetectable amounts of micro-organisms.

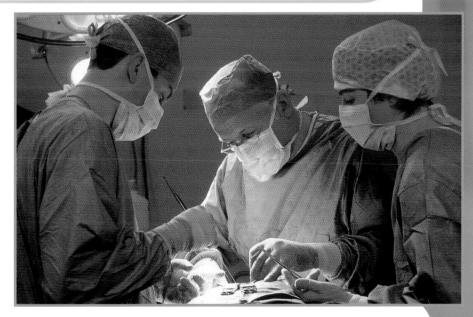

All the equipment in a hospital operating theatre has to be completely sterilized, including the gowns. The medical team wear face masks to prevent micro-organisms from their mouths and noses reaching the patient.

Natural defences

Despite the large number of disease-causing organisms with which we come into contact, we rarely develop diseases. This is because the body is protected by natural barriers such as the skin, **membranes** in the nose and mouth, and secretions such as tears and saliva. And even if these micro-organisms manage to get inside the body, the **immune system** is normally ready to fight them. Without these defences, we would continually suffer from disease and would die.

No entry

The skin forms a physical barrier. Cells in the outermost layer of skin are dead and contain very little water. This makes conditions unpleasant for bacteria and so they are not attracted to these cells. Inside our nasal tubes there are tiny hairs, called cilia, that filter the air we breathe as it passes through the tubes. The cells that line the windpipe produce a sticky mucus that traps any remaining dirt particles and micro-organisms in the air. The mucus is then swept away from the lungs by cilia into the mouth where it is swallowed. Finally, any bacteria that survive the defences they meet in the mouth are finished off by the acidic contents of the stomach.

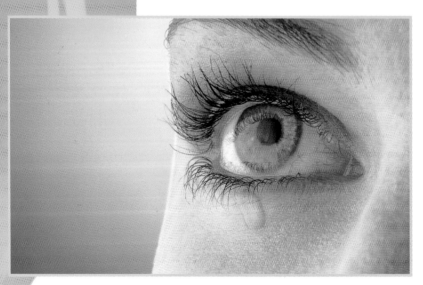

Tears, saliva and sweat all contain chemicals that slow down or stop the growth of bacteria. One chemical is the **enzyme** lysozyme. Lysozyme attacks the walls of bacterial cells.

Our bodies also gain protection from many types of harmless bacteria. These bacteria live on our skin and in our nose, mouth and intestines. Some of their secretions will kill other bacteria. Unfortunately, the various drugs that we use to kill harmful bacteria can also act against these useful ones.

Protection from blood cells

There are two kinds of white blood cells that are responsible for killing micro-organisms: phagocytes and lymphocytes.

Phagocytes

Phagocytes actively seek out foreign particles, either in the blood or in the tissues. When a phagocyte finds a bacterium, it surrounds and absorbs it. The bacterium is killed and then digested. If part of the animal's body becomes infected, the phagocytes move to the infected area and attack the bacteria. The infection site becomes swollen and sore. A thick yellow liquid called pus may collect. Pus contains the bodies of dead bacteria and phagocytes. The inflammation subsides once all the invading bacteria have been killed.

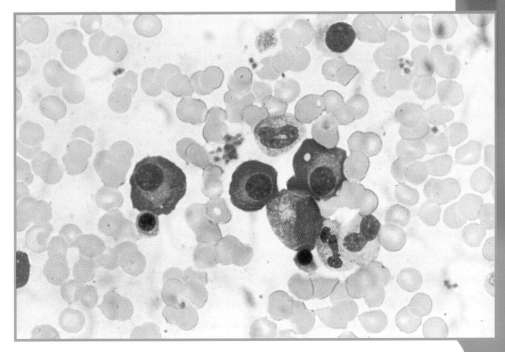

The most numerous cell found in blood is the red blood cell, shown here in grey. There are several types of white blood cell. The large, rounded blue cell in the centre is a lymphocyte that produces antibodies. The white blood cell with an irregular shaped nucleus is a phagocyte.

Lymphocytes

When bacteria invade the bloodstream, they are detected by two types of lymphocyte. One type attacks the bacteria directly, the other releases chemicals called **antibodies**, which attack the bacteria. Antibodies reduce the ability of bacteria to invade the body's cells. Some punch holes in the bacterial walls, causing the contents to leak out. Others stick to the surface of the bacteria, making it easier for the phagocytes to engulf them. Antibodies can make bacteria clump together, preventing them from spreading around the body.

There may not be enough lymphocytes and antibodies at first, so not all of the bacteria may be killed. The surviving bacteria multiply and the person feels unwell. This is because the bacteria are attacking and damaging cells. Eventually more antibodies are produced and all of the bacteria are killed.

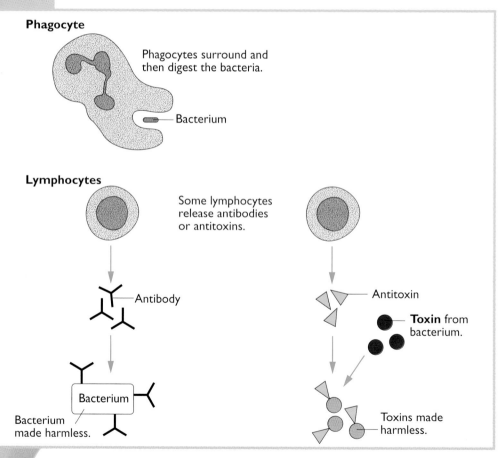

Phagocyte

Phagocytes surround and then digest the bacteria.

Bacterium

Lymphocytes

Some lymphocytes release antibodies or antitoxins.

Antibody

Antitoxin

Toxin from bacterium.

Bacterium

Bacterium made harmless.

Toxins made harmless.

Phagocytes and lymphocytes are two forms of white blood cell. They protect the body in different ways. Phagocytes engulf micro-organisms while lymphocytes produce antibodies and antitoxins.

Developing immunity

The lymphocytes identify their targets from the substances on their target's surface. These surface substances are proteins called **antigens**. Antigens are present on all cells, including bacteria and viruses. The lymphocytes know which antigens are found on their body's own cells and ignore them. Bacterial and viral antigens are different and the lymphocytes recognize them as being foreign. Once a particular antigen has been identified, lymphocytes produce a specific antibody that works only against that antigen. The helpful bacteria that are found on the skin and in our gut are unaffected because they cannot be reached by the lymphocytes.

Natural immunity

Once you have had a childhood disease such as measles or **chickenpox**, you do not get it again. You become **immune** to that disease. During the illness, your lymphocytes learn to recognize the invading antigens and produce a specific type of antibody to destroy it. Should the same type of bacterium or virus attack your body again, the right antibody would immediately be produced in large quantities so you would not get the disease. With some diseases, immunity lasts for life, but with others it may only last a few years or even months. There are some diseases for which we never gain immunity. These include the common cold and **flu**. The virus that causes flu is always changing so it becomes impossible to produce antibodies against all the different forms.

Passive immunity

An unborn baby gets protection against certain diseases from its mother. During pregnancy, some of the mother's antibodies pass across the **placenta** into the unborn baby's blood. The antibodies are also present in the mother's milk, so breast-feeding gives the young baby much greater protection than bottle-feeding. However, this protection is only short-lived. The baby's lymphocytes do not have the information to make new antibodies, so when the antibodies have all been broken down they cannot be replaced. However, this temporary protection is enough to give the baby time to develop its own immune system. This form of immunity is called passive immunity.

Treating disease

One hundred years ago there were few drugs available to treat **infectious** diseases and millions died from their infections or from infections which became **septic**. Today there is a wide range of drugs and the most important are, without doubt, the **antibiotics** which work against bacteria and **fungi**.

Antibiotics

Antibiotics first became available during World War II when these so-called 'wonder drugs' were used to treat wounded soldiers. The very first antibiotic was penicillin, a substance produced by a fungus called *Penicillium*. There are now thousands of different antibiotics, but only 100 or so are widely used.

Antibiotics have selective toxicity. This means that they work only against the bacteria or fungi and not the organism suffering from the disease. A low concentration of an antibiotic is sufficient to slow down the growth of micro-organisms and kill them. Antibiotics are characterized by their effectiveness and their mode of action. Narrow-spectrum antibiotics such as vancomycin are effective against one or two specific types of bacteria, while broad-spectrum antibiotics, for example chloramphenicol and the tetracyclines, work against a wide range of bacteria. Antibiotics differ in the way

While Alexander Fleming was carrying out research into bacteria, he made a chance observation that lead to the discovery of penicillin in 1928.

that they work. Some weaken the bacterial cell wall so that the contents of the cell leak out. Some bind to some of the cell contents and prevent the bacteria from making protein. This slows down bacterial growth and eventually results in their death. Others work against the bacterial cell **membrane**. However, it is important to remember that antibiotics work only against bacteria and fungi. They are completely ineffective against viruses.

Which antibiotic?

In order to determine which antibiotic to use, laboratory tests are carried out. A swab is wiped over the infected part of the patient and smeared over the surface of sterile agar in a Petri dish. Agar is a jelly-like substance that contains nutrients for the bacteria. Then small, circular, sterile discs of filter paper, each saturated with a different antibiotic, are placed on the agar, spaced equally apart. The plate is covered with a lid and placed in an incubator at 37°C for 24 hours. The plate is then examined. If the antibiotic has been effective there will be a clear zone under and around the disc where the antibiotic has spread out and destroyed the bacteria. Antibiotics that are not effective will be surrounded by bacterial growth.

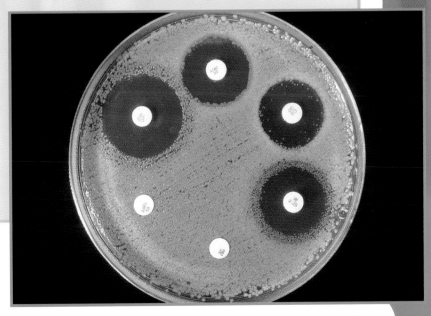

The clear areas around four of the discs indicate that the antibiotics on these discs were effective against *E.coli* bacteria. However, two antibiotics failed to prevent the growth of these bacteria.

Over-use

Over the last 50 years, the prescribing (giving) of antibiotics has risen dramatically, but much of this has been unnecessary. Health experts estimate that doctors are both over-prescribing and incorrectly prescribing, either in the type or the amount of the drug that is given. Far too often antibiotics are given to people suffering from viral diseases, on which the antibiotics will have no effect. People are as much to blame as doctors. Many people still feel that their doctor hasn't treated their illness unless they have been given some antibiotics. They would rather have a quick 'fix' for a minor infection than put up with some discomfort for a few days.

Antibiotics are also used widely in intensively farmed livestock systems. The antibiotics keep the animals healthier and so they produce more muscle. They are added to the animals' food, even if the animals do not show any signs of illness. Sometimes, antibiotics can be detected in food products such as meat.

Resistance

The excessive use of antibiotics is threatening the future use of these drugs. Bacteria continually change their genetic make-up. Any changes (called mutations) in their genetic content is passed on to new generations when they reproduce. Some of these mutations give bacteria **resistance** to antibiotics. Bacteria that are penicillin-resistant have a **gene** that allows them to produce an **enzyme** that breaks down the antibiotic, making it ineffective. The bacteria that have the gene survive the antibiotic treatment. When they reproduce, they pass their resistance genes on to generations of new bacteria. The resistance quickly spreads through the bacterial populations.

It is important that patients take the whole of a course of antibiotics. Sometimes, they feel better after a few days and stop the treatment. If this happens, there is a possibility that some of the bacteria will survive. These bacteria may be more difficult to kill if they are treated with the same antibiotic in the future.

Antibiotics are relatively expensive, so in countries where there is no state medical care, only a small number of people can afford them. This has led to an illegal trade by unqualified people. Often people cannot afford the whole course so only buy half the number of tablets needed to kill all the bacteria, which simply contributes to the bacteria's strength. Also, there are a lot of poor quality antibiotics, produced by unlicensed drug companies, which do not work well.

Multi-resistant bacteria

Partly as a result of the misuse of antibiotics, bacteria have emerged that are now resistant to several different types of antibiotics. When this happens the bacteria are very difficult to kill. A patient infected with a resistant strain of bacterium has a prolonged illness and may stay in hospital for longer. They remain infectious for longer and there is a greater chance that they will die. They have to be treated with alternative drugs, which could be expensive and may cause side effects. One bacterium causing concern is MRSA or methicillin-resistant *Staphylococcus aureus* – a bacterium that is commonly found in hospitals. Patients who are most susceptible are those who have open wounds as a result of surgery. MRSA infects the patients, causing the healing process to slow down, which increases the possibility that the wounds will become infected. This bacteria was once controlled by penicillin, but now only ten per cent of patients respond to this treatment.

'Antibiotic resistance as a phenomenon is, in itself, not surprising. Nor is it new. It is, however, newly worrying because it is accumulating and accelerating, while the world's tools for combating it decrease in power and number.'
Joshua Lederberg, Nobel Prize winner

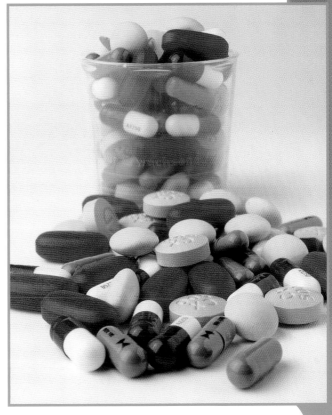

There is a wide range of antibiotics on sale. Some are in the form of tablets, while others are capsules.

The return of tuberculosis

Tuberculosis (TB) was once considered a disease of the past, but it has returned and now the World Health Organization has declared it a global emergency. Millions of people contract the disease each year. Most of the cases are in developing countries, but the disease is now reappearing in developed countries.

Airborne TB bacteria enter the lungs, where they may persist for years without actually causing the disease. Then suddenly, the body's **immune system** fails and the bacteria start to grow and reproduce. The reasons for this system failure are unclear, but it may be linked to a person's general health and whether they are experiencing stress. The bacteria form balls (called tubercules), which block some of the tubes leading into the lungs. Every time an infected person sneezes, coughs or even breathes out, they spread bacteria into the air.

TB can be treated, but the treatment involves a six- to eight-month course of drugs. Many people stop part-way through because they feel better and this allows the bacteria to survive and spread. This has led to the emergence of multidrug-resistant TB. This disease was relatively cheap to treat. However, the emergence of antibiotic-resistant bacteria means that other, much more expensive drugs have to be used.

This TB sufferer must take every dose of anti-TB drugs in front of a health worker. This is to ensure that the course of drugs is completed.

*'Everyone who breathes air, from Wall Street to the Great Wall of China, needs to worry about this risk. Once multidrug-resistant TB is unleashed, we may never be able to stop it. We will face a deadly infectious disease that spreads through the air, yet is virtually as incurable as **AIDS** or **Ebola**. This frightening prospect must be avoided at any cost!'*

Statement released by the WHO

Friend or foe?

Our intestines are populated by a harmless bacterium called *Escherichia coli* or *E.coli*. However, new strains are emerging that cause severe food poisoning. In Scotland in 1996, a new strain of *E.coli* O157 caused an outbreak of food poisoning, affecting 582 people and killing 21. The bacterium proved to be difficult to control as it was resistant to a range of antibiotics. During the 1990s similar outbreaks occurred in the USA killing children and adults.

Keeping some back

The way forward is to reduce the number of antibiotics in use so that fewer bacteria are exposed to them. There are a few antibiotics that doctors are asked not to prescribe. These antibiotics are kept back and only used as a last resort. This means that bacteria are rarely exposed to these antibiotics or given the chance to develop resistance.

Alternatives

There are few alternatives to antibiotics. One controversial treatment is colloidal silver. Silver is described as a heavy metal and can be toxic if taken into the body. However, under certain circumstances silver can be used medically. It is prepared as a colloidal suspension, which means that ultra-fine particles of silver are suspended by an electrical charge in purified water. The electric charge prevents the particles from sinking. This preparation has been found to have antibacterial properties. Doctors report that, taken internally, it can work against **syphilis** and **cholera**. However, national authorities, including the US Federal Drug Authority, are investigating the claims made about this treatment before making it available.

Animals such as frogs and toads suffer few diseases. This may be due to chemicals in their skin which kill bacteria and other micro-organisms. Research is underway to identify these chemicals and see if they can be used medically.

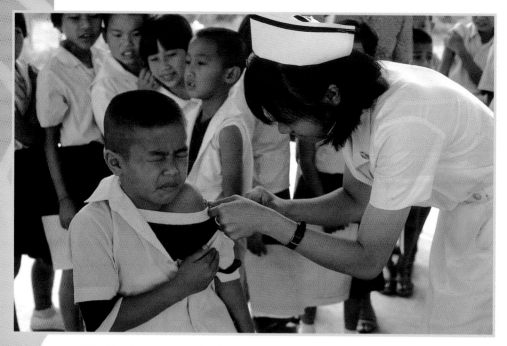

Worldwide, mass vaccination progammes protect school children from a number of serious diseases.

Vaccination

The immunity described on page 21 is naturally acquired as a result of the body being exposed to a particular micro-organism. A similar immune response can be stimulated artificially. This involves injecting **antigens** into the body in a process known as **vaccination**. A **vaccine** is a small quantity of antigen that is either injected or swallowed, the antigen having been made harmless first. Once inside the body, it triggers an immune response. The body then produces **antibodies** in the same way as if there were bacteria or viruses present.

Nowadays, doctors vaccinate people against a whole range of diseases and there are several types of vaccines (see table on page 29). Some vaccines, for example the **whooping cough** and cholera vaccines, contain dead bacteria or viruses that have been killed by heat or chemicals. Others contain weakened micro-organisms. Weakening the organism prevents it from causing the disease, but its presence in the body is enough to stimulate antibody production. Examples include a **polio** vaccine, which is taken orally, and the BCG vaccine against TB. The bacteria that cause **diphtheria** and **tetanus** release a **toxin**. It is the toxin that causes the disease. Vaccines have been developed to work against these toxins. The toxin is made harmless and used in the vaccine.

The following table lists the world's major diseases, the infectious agent that causes them, their symptoms and the type of vaccine used to combat them.

Disease	Causative agent and method of transmission	Symptoms	Type of vaccine
AIDS	**HIV** virus, spread by hypodermic needles, sexual intercourse, contaminated blood products and across the **placenta**	Attacks a type of white blood cell called T-helper or T4 cells, destroying immune system	No vaccine
Cholera	*Vibrio cholerae* bacterium, transmitted via water or food contaminated with human **faeces**	Toxins from the bacteria inflame intestinal wall, causing severe diarrhoea, dehydration	Vaccine of killed bacteria
Common cold	Rhinovirus, spread by touch	Attacks upper **respiratory** tract, causing sneezing, coughing	No effective vaccine
Hepatitis B	Virus, spread by blood contact	Attacks liver, causes **jaundice**	**Genetically engineered** vaccine
Measles	Rubeola bacterium, spread by droplets	Fever, rash, cough	Weakened virus
Meningitis C	Meningococcus bacterium, spread by droplets in the air	Attacks the membranes around the brain, causes high fever and rash	Vaccine that combines sugar-based compounds from the bacterial wall with a protein
Mumps	Paramyxovirus, spread by droplets	Fever, headache, swelling of salivary glands	Weakened virus
Poliomyelitis or polio	Poliovirus, spread by droplets and faeces	Attacks nerve fibres, leading to paralysis and muscle wastage	Weakened virus (given orally on sugar lump) or dead/inactivated virus (injected)
Rubella or German measles	Rubella virus, spread by droplets	Attacks respiratory passage and lymph nodes, crosses placenta and damages unborn child	Weakened virus (usually given with mumps and measles in the MMR vaccine)
Smallpox (now extinct)	Variola virus	Fever, rash	Weakened virus
Tetanus	*Clostridium tetani* bacterium, from soil or dung into deep wounds	Violent muscular spasms preventing breathing and drinking	Preventative vaccine of inactivated toxin, boosters needed. Immediate treatment of infection with **serum** containing antibodies.
Tuberculosis (TB)	*Mycobacterium tuberculosis* bacterium, spread by droplets or contaminated milk	Affects the lungs and causes loss of body weight	Weakened bacteria
Whooping cough	*Bordetella pertussis* bacterium, spread by droplets	Severe coughing in young children, with characteristic 'whoop' sound	Dead/inactivated bacteria

Some vaccines give protection for life. However, protection against diseases such as **typhoid** and cholera is short-lived, so the vaccination must be repeated at intervals. These vaccinations are called boosters.

The **flu** vaccine is different to others. It contains a selection of antigens that have been removed from several different forms of the virus. It has been found that just the presence of part of a virus, rather than the whole virus, is enough to trigger the immune response.

Some of the latest vaccines have been producing by genetic engineering, for example the **hepatitis** B vaccine. Other genetically engineered vaccines are in the pipeline.

Vaccine manufacture

The bacterial cells used in vaccines are grown in large vats or fermenters. They are provided with ideal conditions, so they grow and divide rapidly. The bacteria are then treated in a number of ways

Homeopathic remedies are available for most diseases. A homeopathic practitioner will decide which remedy to use by carefully studying the symptoms displayed by the patient.

depending on the type of vaccine being made. Genetic engineering is used increasingly in vaccine manufacture. The genes responsible for the antigen production in disease-causing organisms are identified and transferred to a less dangerous organisms such as the bacterium *E.coli*. The genetically engineered bacteria are grown in fermenters and harvested. The antigen is extracted from the cell debris. A genetically engineered vaccine causes fewer side affects as the vaccine is purer and safer than a vaccine prepared traditionally. For example, there is a minute chance that in a vaccine containing dead bacteria, there may be a few living ones or that weakened bacteria may regain their pathogenic (disease-causing) properties.

Homeopathic medicines

Homeopathic medicine is based on the principle that the symptoms of disease are part of the body's self-healing processes. The Greek word *homoios* means 'similar' and *pathos* means 'disease' or 'suffering'. Homeopathic practitioners use various minerals or extracts of plants or animals in very small doses to stimulate a sick person's natural defences. The theory is that the medicines work with the body's defences, rather than against them.

First, homeopathic practitioners learn about the symptoms that appear when a homeopathic substance is given in overdose to a healthy person. Then they interview their patients in great detail to discover all the physical, emotional and mental symptoms the person is experiencing. They look for a substance that will cause similar symptoms and then give it in a small, specially prepared dose. In many cases, there are alternative remedies available for a disease and the choice depends on the symptoms displayed by the patient. For example, a person suffering from **chickenpox** may have such severe itching that they cannot stop scratching, in which case the best remedy is the plant *Rhus toxicodendron*. However, if the patient is hot and feverish, has a red flushed face and their eyes are sensitive to light, the better remedy is the belladonna plant.

Homeopathy has been used for hundreds of years, all around the world and especially in India. Until recently, the great majority of doctors were sceptical about its benefits. However, in recent years its popularity has increased considerably. There are many specialist homeopathic doctors and in addition, many family doctors are choosing to use homeopathic remedies alongside conventional ones.

Discovering new drugs

Although there is a wide range of drugs available to treat **infectious** diseases, drug companies are always looking for new ones. This ongoing research and development is essential, as disease-causing organisms develop **resistance** to the current treatments.

A wide range of plant and animal species, many of which are unknown to science, will be found in just this small area of tropical rainforest. These species could be potential sources of new drugs.

Valuable plants

Plants have long been used medicinally. About one-third of the existing drugs are derived from plants and **fungi**. The top drug plants, financially, are the yam (steroids for contraceptive pills), poppy (painkillers such as codeine) and deadly nightshade (nerve drugs such as atropine).

Many drug companies have programmes to screen plants for useful compounds. Scientists visit habitats such as rainforests and remote mountains to find new plants. They also spend time with tribal peoples to learn about the traditional drugs that they use, most of which are derived from plants. Native Americans used a coneflower to treat **respiratory** illnesses, while people on the Caribbean island of Martinique use hibiscus and begonia to treat **flu**. The drug quinine, which is used to treat **malaria**, is obtained from the bark of the cinchona tree. The rosy periwinkle, a plant found in the rainforests of Madagascar, was found to be effective against various forms of leukaemia (cancer of white blood cells). However, few plant-based drugs are extracted from commercially grown plants. Instead they are taken from wild plants. This means that the availability can vary as a result of weather conditions, political unrest or over-exploitation, which may cause the plant to become endangered. Research is taking place into ways in which these drug plants can be grown commercially under controlled conditions to obtain a high-quality product that provides an all-year-round supply.

Botanicals

There are now several companies specializing in the development of pharmaceutical products from plant extracts. Initially these companies are focusing on plants that have been used in traditional medicines. They produce extracts of the plants, which are called botanicals. These extracts may not be pure but a mix of several different substances. Often this mix can enhance the medicinal effect. This is different to traditional research, where the individual substances in a plant are identified and isolated – a lengthy process. Companies working with botanicals carry out tests on the extract, which is far simpler, so they can move on to clinical trials more quickly. Many diseases are poorly understood, so new approaches, such as the use of botanicals, are needed.

Development costs

Finding a potential source of a new drug is just the first stage. Every drug that is prescribed has to go through an extensive testing process. The development of a new drug is expensive and time consuming. The costs are very high, as much as US$500 million per drug, and it can be as long as ten years before it is proved to be effective and safe to sell. Many promising products fail to reach the shelves because of the tremendous costs involved. Only one in 1000 compounds that enter pre-clinical testing get to the stage of human testing. Then there is just a one in five chance that it will be approved for sale.

> 'Often we consciously search for a drug for a specific use, but more often it is serendipity [luck]. What is required, though, is good science building on good science.'
> Clement Stone, a former senior vice president for Merck and Co. Inc.
> research laboratories, USA

One of the first stages in drug development is the production of a potential drug, which then undergoes extensive testing.

Stages in the drug development process

Stage 1 Pre-clinical testing

Up to three years. A drug company conducts laboratory and animal studies to investigate the way the compound works against the targeted disease, and the compound is evaluated for safety.

Stage 2 Clinical trials

There are usually three phases of clinical trial:

Phase I – One year. These tests involve between 20 and 80 normal, healthy volunteers. The tests determine what is a safe dosage (amount taken at one time), how the drug is absorbed, distributed, broken down and excreted by the body, and the length of time it remains active in the body.

Phase II – Two years. In this phase, the drug's effectiveness is assessed through controlled studies of approximately 100 to 300 volunteer patients who have the disease.

Phase III – Three years. This phase involves between 1000 and 3000 patients in clinics and hospitals. Doctors monitor the patients closely to determine the efficiency of the drug and to identify any side effects.

Stage 3 Request for approval

Up to two years. Following the completion of all the clinical trials, the company has to submit all their results to the relevant drug authority. The drug authority reviews the information and decides whether to approve the drug or not.

Stage 4 Approval

Once the drug is approved for use, it becomes available for doctors to prescribe. However, the drug company continues to submit reports to the drug authority, including any cases of adverse reactions.

The pre-clinical tests

The first stage is to study how the body functions, both when healthy and when suffering from the disease. Disease processes are complex and involve a sequence of events. Scientists have to break down the process into its component parts and then analyse these to find out what abnormal events are occurring. They select a particular step in the disease process as a target for drug development, with the aim of correcting the abnormality. Once the target has been identified they have to find a drug that might work in the desired way. Literally hundreds and sometimes thousands of compounds must be tested to find one that can achieve the desirable result without serious side effects.

Until this point in the testing process, the search for a new drug has been confined to a laboratory test tube. Next, scientists have to test the promising compounds in living animals. In animal testing, drug companies make every effort to use as few animals as possible and to ensure their humane and proper care. Two or more species are

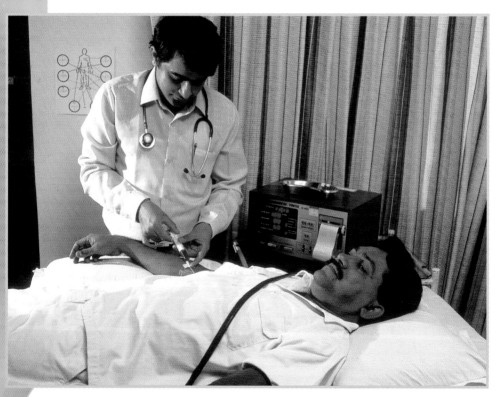

During a clinical trial, doctors have to make detailed notes on the patient's response to the new treatment. The trial is stopped as soon as any adverse effect is noted.

typically tested, since a drug may affect one differently from another. Such tests show whether a potential drug has toxic (poisonous) side effects and at what level it can be used safely.

By this time in the testing process, many drugs that had seemed promising have been abandoned because they are unsafe, poorly absorbed by the blood, or simply don't work. Sometimes drugs may be put to one side because they failed to work on one disease, only to be 'rediscovered' years later when they are found to work on another. This happened with the drug AZT (also called zidovudine), which is given to **AIDS** patients. The drug was first studied in 1964 as an anti-cancer drug, but it showed little promise. It was not until the 1980s, when searches began for AIDS treatments, that scientists found it had very positive results in human testing. It was finally approved for use in the USA in 1987.

Clinical trials

The next stage is clinical trials, where the drugs are tested on humans. To be sure that the drug is effective, not all the patients will receive the new drug. There are usually two groups of patients. One group receives the drug under investigation. The second group, called the control group, undergoes one of the following: no treatment at all; a **placebo**; another drug known to be effective. The results from one group are compared with the other. The trials are set up just like an experiment. There is one variable, the drug. All the other variables have to be kept as constant as possible. This means that all the individuals involved in the trials have to be as similar as possible, for example of the same age, weight, and general health status. They should all have the disease which is under study and be at the same stage of the disease. The individuals are randomly placed in either the treatment or control group, so that there is no bias.

Approval

The national drug authority will examine the results of the clinical trials and decide whether the drug can be sold to the public. During the testing process the results are continually monitored, and the trial can be stopped if it is thought that the people receiving the drug are being harmed by it. In a few cases the drug may prove to be so successful that the trial is stopped early and approval sought, so that more people can benefit. This happened with the AZT trials of the 1980s. Doctors noticed the improved survival rate for patients receiving AZT, the trial was ended early and permission was given for more than 4000 patients to receive AZT before it was approved for marketing.

Drugs: issues today
AIDS in South Africa

More than 20 per cent of the population of South Africa has been infected with **HIV**. Unfortunately, the health service cannot afford to buy the AIDS drugs, such as AZT, that extend the lives of people infected with the virus. These drugs are protected by patents and they cannot be manufactured without a licence. A patent is protection given to a new invention, process or drug, that allows the patent-holder exclusive rights to the invention for 20 years. During that period other people may not use the invention without permission from the patent-holder. All drug companies protect their drugs in this way. They invest so much in their development that they have to recoup this money (and make a profit!) by selling them. No company would spend millions of pounds on drug development if they knew a competitor could come along and copy their drug for nothing. However, the South African government threatened to ignore the patents and produce the AIDS drugs without licence, in order to provide their people with cheap drugs. The case went to court and in 2001 the verdict went in the South African government's favour. This shows the dilemma faced by the drug companies – they cannot afford to give away the drugs as they

need income to finance future research. But the people in greatest need of the drugs cannot afford them. The way forward is probably a compromise, whereby the drug companies allow the drugs to be manufactured under a licence, but at a price that South Africa and other African countries can afford.

Bacterial **cultures** can be stored at very low temperatures until they are required for research. This is called cryostorage.

Fighting malaria

A **vaccine** against **malaria** is desperately needed. Although research is under way, it is proving to be quite a challenge. The disease-causing organism is a **protozoan** called plasmodium. Its biology is very similar to that of a human cell so it is difficult to find a target for the vaccine that does not have any side effects.

When developing any new vaccine, certain features are essential. It should:
- be safe and easy to manufacture
- be easy to administer
- provide life-long **immunity** against all forms of the disease.

The ideal malaria vaccine would prevent infection by stimulating the **immune system** to destroy all the **parasites**, at all stages in their life cycle. Unfortunately this is extremely difficult to achieve and might not be technically feasible. One problem is the very 'clever' nature of the parasite. It has evolved a series of strategies that allow it to confuse, hide, and misdirect the human immune system. Many vaccine developers have therefore focused their efforts on creating a vaccine that limits the parasite's ability to successfully infect large numbers of red blood cells. This would not prevent infection, but would limit the severity of the disease and help prevent malaria deaths. Once a vaccine has been developed, the next important stage will be to ensure that it is given to all the people who need it, especially the people most at risk in developing countries.

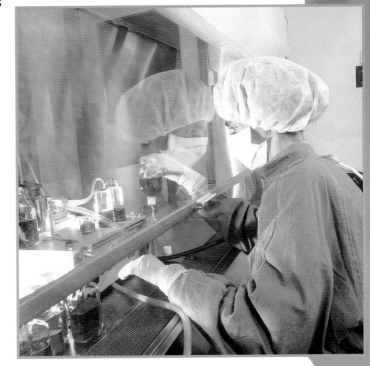

Research into viral diseases takes place under very carefully controlled conditions. Here, all the experimental cultures containing viruses are kept in an isolation cupboard so that there can be no accidental contamination of the atmosphere.

Preventing the spread of disease

Over the last 50 years, the incidence of some of the major diseases such as **polio** and **diphtheria** and some parasitic diseases has fallen significantly. **Smallpox** has been completely **eradicated**. This has been due to **vaccination** programmes, improvements in community and personal hygiene and better food supply. People who are well-fed, clean and healthy are less likely to succumb to disease.

Epidemics and pandemics

In any group of people there will always be a few individuals who are suffering from an infection. When a few individuals in a small area suffer from the same disease in a short period of time it is called an outbreak. An epidemic is when a large number of people from several communities suffer from the same infection. And finally, a pandemic is when a large number of people from a wide geographical area suffer from the same infection.

Several factors contribute to the global spread of an **infectious** disease. First, it depends on how easily the

Fighting meningitis C

Meningitis is a disease that affects the brain. There are several forms of the disease, some bacterial and others viral, but the most serious is meningitis C, a viral form. In its early stage the disease resembles flu, but the symptoms worsen and the individual develops a high fever. One in ten sufferers die from the disease. During the 1990s there was a massive increase in the incidence of meningitis C, which mostly affects under 24-year-olds. By 1998, the C form accounted for 40 per cent of all cases of the disease and there were 150 deaths in the USA alone. In 1999, a new vaccine was introduced in the UK and it has proved to be highly successful. Within one year, the incidence of meningitis C had dropped by approximately 75 per cent. The vaccination programme aims to have all children under eighteen protected against the disease and more than 15 million doses of the vaccine have been issued. The success of this vaccine led to other countries, including the USA, setting up their own programmes in 2001.

disease-causing organism spreads from person to person. For example, the **tuberculosis** (TB) bacterium moves through a population more slowly than the **flu** virus. Human behaviour and public health conditions are also important factors. Re-using needles for injecting **vaccines** or drugs increases risk of infection, as does using water from a polluted source.

Fighting cholera

Cholera is a deadly intestinal disease that causes diarrhoea, abdominal cramps, nausea, vomiting and severe dehydration. It can kill within 24 hours. The bacteria are carried in water and food that has been contaminated with **faeces**. It can also be caught by eating contaminated raw or undercooked seafood. There have been recent epidemics following flooding in Madagascar and Mozambique and typhoons in India. While non-antibiotic treatments are effective against mild forms of the disease, the usual treatment is **antibiotics**, which shorten the duration of the illness. However, many of the antibiotics no longer work. There is a vaccine but it is short-lived and only about 50 per cent effective. However, scientists have recently announced that they now know the genetic code for the bacterium that causes cholera. Experts are optimistic that this knowledge will help in the development of an effective cholera vaccine.

In 1994 a major cholera epidemic broke out in Somalia. It was spread by drinking water contaminated with sewage, and by infected people preparing food. Aid agencies set up emergency medical centres to treat the thousands of people who contracted the disease.

Flu pandemics

The most recent pandemics have been those associated with flu. The 1918–20 flu pandemic killed 20 million people, more people than were killed during World War I. In 1997 there was an outbreak of avian or bird flu in Hong Kong and it was feared that this might be the start of another pandemic. Fortunately, these fears were unfounded, but its appearance was a warning that a pandemic could break out at any time. Flu is caused by a virus that exists in different strains, called A, B and C. The virus undergoes continual change. Epidemics of these strains occur at different intervals. Flu strain A causes major epidemics that sweep across the world every three years or so. Strains B and C cause fewer epidemics. There are vaccines against some strains, but they are only effective for a short time due to the changeable nature of the virus.

Every year, scientists study thousands of samples of flu virus taken from around the world to predict which types are likely to dominate the next flu season. This early information gives the drug companies time to produce a suitable vaccine. There is always the possibility that a pandemic strain could emerge. Such a strain would have the potential

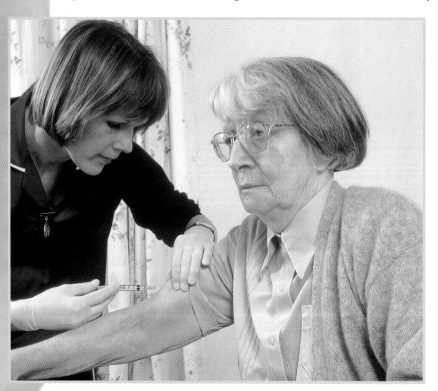

Flu vaccines are usually in short supply so they are normally only given to people at risk such as the elderly, people with respiratory problems, health and care workers.

to spread around the world in months, as international travel is now so commonplace. Health agencies prepare national and international action plans in case a pandemic strain emerges. Once a new strain actually strikes, the public health agencies have to swing into action. They inform the public, educate medical workers and implement their mass vaccination programmes.

'Today, in 30 hours, you can literally travel to the other side of the world. And likewise, while you are there, you can pick up a germ or a micro-organism that may not exist on this side of the globe and within 30 hours you can have that back in the United States.'

US Republican Senator Bill Frist

Hantavirus

Hantavirus is a relatively new strain of virus that appeared out of nowhere. In 1992, in the south-western USA, there was record rainfall and snow, which followed five years of severe drought. As a result, the population of rodents exploded. Unknown to people at the time, the deer mouse was carrying a fatal strain of hantavirus. Healthy people who came into close contact with the deer mouse contracted a deadly **respiratory** disease. Disease experts identified the disease's source as a strain of hantavirus, a type of rodent-related virus. Since 1993, about 150 cases of this respiratory disease have been identified in the USA, and a further 200 in Canada and South America. The disease kills up to half the people who get it. Scientists believe that the weather could have been the key to the sudden emergence of this viral strain.

Vaccination programmes

Vaccination programmes are essential in controlling the spread of disease. Smallpox was successfully eradicated because the disease was easy to identify, the virus did not change and the vaccine was simply applied by scratching the skin rather than through injection. Polio, too, will be eradicated within the next few years. Childhood vaccination programmes have reduced the incidence of diseases such as measles and mumps (see page 29). However, vaccination programmes are only effective if most of the children of a particular age group are vaccinated. If the percentage of children vaccinated falls to below 60 per cent, the disease starts to spread again among the unprotected children.

The MMR vaccine

Measles is a serious disease. In 1998 there were 30 million measles cases worldwide and 1 million measle-related deaths. Between 1989 and 1991, a measles epidemic swept across the USA, infecting 55,000 children and causing 120 deaths. Children are given a triple vaccine known as MMR (measles, mumps and **rubella**) as part of their childhood immunization programme. By 1992, 90 per cent of children in the UK were being immunized and the incidence of these diseases fell sharply.

MMR and autism

It was recently discovered that a tiny number of children became seriously ill within weeks of receiving the MMR vaccination. These children began behaving strangely, stopped talking and became socially withdrawn, staring into space for hours on end. These are symptoms of a condition known as autism, which is characterized by a reduced ability to respond to or communicate with the outside world. There is now considerable debate about a possible link between the vaccine and autism. There have been several studies, but their results have been conflicting. There is no doubt that the incidence of autism in the UK and USA over the last ten years has increased sharply. So is this a causal link or just a coincidence? The first symptoms of autism usually show themselves when a child is about three years old, the same age at which they receive a second dose of MMR. So it is possible that it is just a coincidence. Autism is difficult to diagnose and in the past the symptoms may have gone unnoticed. Today, doctors and parents are far more aware of the condition and so more children are being diagnosed.

It is also possible that environmental and dietary changes could be involved. Over the last few decades there has been an increase in the range and quantity of pollutants in the air, water and on land, some of which are known to affect the unborn child. Also, the diet of people in developed countries has changed, with a shift to protein and fat-rich foods and processed foods. Some autistic children have shown an improvement in their symptoms once dairy produce and wheat gluten were removed from their diets.

Fewer vaccinations

Now MMR vaccination rates are falling as parents and some doctors decide not to vaccinate. If the rate falls any further, there is a risk that there will be a measles epidemic. Parents are faced with a difficult choice. Do they decide that the risk of autism is very small and go ahead with the vaccination, thereby protecting both their own children and the population as a whole against measles? Or do they decide the risk is too great to vaccinate? If they decide the risk is too great, they are putting their children and the rest of the unvaccinated population at greater risk of contracting measles.

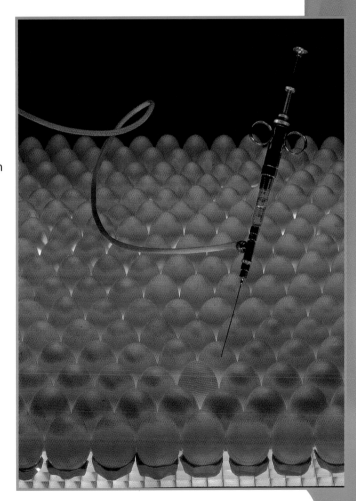

Viruses can only be **cultured** in living cells. A convenient source is fertilized hens' eggs. Eggs are inoculated with the virus using a fine needle. The egg highlighted in the photograph has just been inoculated. The viruses multiply within the eggs and a week or so later they are harvested. The viruses are either modified or killed and used in vaccines.

Controlling parasites

The best way to tackle parasitic diseases is to target the vector – the organism that transmits the disease-causing organism. If the **parasite** loses its means of transmission then the infection rates will fall. It is important to understand the life cycle of the parasite and its vector. For example, the female mosquito (vector) lays her eggs on the surface of small pools and ponds where the water is often stagnant. The larvae hatch and live in the water until they pupate and turn into adults. Adult mosquitoes can be killed by spraying them with insecticides (chemicals that kill insect pests). The larvae can be killed by spraying oil on the water's surface. Another, cheaper method is to stock the ponds with fish that eat the larvae. However, to be successful all of these methods have to be used. It is also important to stop the mosquitoes from biting people. Fine mesh screens over doors and windows and mosquito-nets over beds keep the insects from getting too close. People can also avoid being bitten by using insect-repellents and covering their arms and legs at dusk when the insects are most active.

Bilharzia

Bilharzia is a parasitic disease caused by a fluke, a type of flat worm. More than 200 million people worldwide are infected with this parasite. It lives part of its life in a human host and most of the rest of its life in a type of water snail. People become infected with the parasite when they come into contact with fresh water in which the contaminated water snail (host) is living. The parasites grow and develop inside the snails and then leave them, entering the water. They can survive in the water, without a host, for about 48 hours. During

Return of DDT

During the 1960s a new pesticide, DDT, was used to kill insect pests. But there was a problem – DDT did not break down and it was taken up into the bodies of animals when they ate plants and insects sprayed with the pesticide. This resulted in the deaths of many millions of birds and mammals. As a result of the terrible side effects, DDT was banned by most countries. However, it was a very effective treatment against mosquitoes. It was sprayed on ponds and over walls and roofs of houses and the incidence of **malaria** fell. Now many organizations are asking that DDT be used again, despite its effects on the environment. They argue that it is needed because malaria is on the increase. DDT is easy to apply and relatively cheap, enabling poor people to protect their homes. What is more important – the health of millions of people or the environment?

this time they can infect anyone who is wading, swimming, bathing or washing in the water by penetrating their skin. Within several weeks, the flukes grow (up to 2 cm long) inside the blood vessels of the body and produce eggs. Some of these eggs travel to the bladder or intestines and are passed into the urine or faeces. The cycle of contamination continues if the infected person's urine or faeces enters and contaminates fresh water.

One area where a successful prevention programme has taken place is Lake Malawi in Africa. Since the programme was started in 1989, the local infection rates have fallen from 40 per cent to 14 per cent. The infection rate in children was even higher – 80 per cent – and now this has fallen by half. Studies showed that 40 per cent of the population had no toilets, and over 65 per cent had no access to safe drinking water. The project launched health education campaigns, drilled bore-holes for safer drinking water and taught villagers to construct pit toilets. Also, massive over-fishing in the lake had caused the fish population to fall. As the fish feed on these water snails, the lower numbers meant that more snails survived. So it was important to reduce the snail population another way. There are chemicals which kill the snails, but a natural source of poison was recently found in a local type of plant. This fast-growing plant is now grown commercially and its extract can be added to the water to kill the snails.

One approach to the control of malaria is to spray insecticides over the surfaces where mosquitoes can be found, such as walls and paths around buildings.

Containing the outbreaks

In the past, one of the most effective ways of preventing the spread of disease was the use of hospital isolation wards. This meant that patients suffering from **infectious** diseases were kept separate from other patients, thereby reducing the spread of the disease. The nursing staff wore protective clothing, and doors into these wards were sealed to stop the disease-causing organisms from escaping. These forms of treatment are less common today as there are more vaccines and drug treatments available. However, **Ebola** is one disease that still has to be treated using isolation.

Ebola haemorrhagic fever is a severe, often fatal disease in humans that spreads very rapidly. Typically it appears in sporadic outbreaks in central Africa. Humans do not carry the virus so it is likely that the first case is caused after contact with an infected animal. The initial symptoms are fever, headache, stomach pain, vomiting blood and bloody diarrhoea. Within one week, the disease progresses to chest pain, shock, blindness and bleeding. Death is the most common outcome.

The first case in an outbreak is called the index case. At this point, the virus can spread in several ways. Family, friends and nursing staff caring for the sufferer may come into contact with blood or body secretions, or touch needles that have been contaminated with infected secretions. In African health-care facilities, patients are often cared for without the use of a mask, gown or gloves, so nursing staff are exposed to the virus. Non-disposable needles and syringes may be used without adequate **sterilization**. If needles or syringes become contaminated with the virus and are then re-used, many people can become infected. The only way to combat the disease is to isolate the patients or even whole communities to prevent contact with other people and to let the disease run its course. Often teams of experts come in to oversee the control procedure. These people come from agencies such as the Centers for Disease Control and Prevention (CDC) in the USA (see panel), and they have both the necessary experience and equipment that the local people may lack.

'With each outbreak, we know a little bit more. This virus is spread a lot like another virus, **Hepatitis** B, which is spread through mainly contact with blood. We also know that the virus does attack chimpanzees and kills chimpanzees as well as humans. But we still don't know where the virus hides in nature.'

David Heymann of the World Heath Organization, talking about the Ebola outbreak in Zaire in 1996

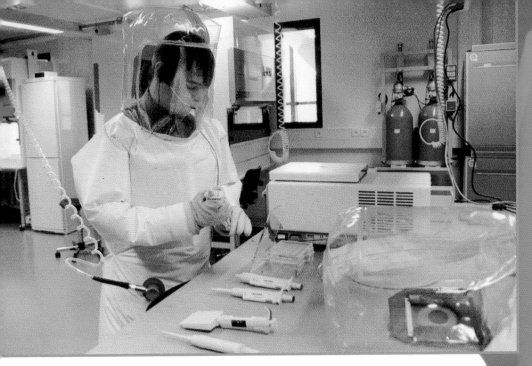

Ebola is such a deadly disease that researchers working on it have to wear protective suits and breathe air that comes from outside the research laboratory to avoid becoming infected.

Centers for Disease Control and Prevention (CDC)

The CDC is the leading federal agency in the USA for protecting the health and safety of people, both at home and abroad. The agency is located in Atlanta, Georgia and serves as the national focus for disease prevention and control and environmental health. It undertakes health promotion and education activities that are designed to improve the health of the people living in the USA. The agency was established in 1946 and now has more than 8500 employees across the USA. It also works with partners throughout the world to monitor diseases, especially the newer diseases such as Ebola. New diseases have the potential to spread across the world in a matter of days, even hours, so early detection and rapid action are more important than ever. The CDC plays a critical role in controlling these diseases, sending teams to investigate outbreaks wherever they occur.

Health education

Often it is more important to stop the diseases spreading than to cure them. In some cases, especially viral diseases, there is no cure, so prevention is essential.

AIDS education

During the late 1980s in Europe and North America there were major campaigns to warn people of the dangers of **AIDS**. This disease is caused by the **HIV** virus. A person infected with the virus is described as being HIV-positive. They can remain HIV-positive for many years before the symptoms of AIDS appear. Nowadays there are many drugs available that act to prolong the life of the AIDS sufferer, but there is no cure. The best way to beat AIDS is to stop the virus from spreading. The virus is spread by sexual intercourse, across the **placenta** from mother to unborn child, by blood transfusions, in contaminated blood products including blood-clotting agents used by haemophiliacs, and by sharing needles. Campaigns on television, radio and in newspapers and magazines told people what measures they should take to protect themselves from catching the virus. These

A large AIDS awareness poster by a roadside in Botswana, Africa. This sends a simple message to the population.

campaigns were successful and the number of infected people decreased. However, in recent years there has been a slight increase. The warnings need to be repeated for today's younger generations, who are now at risk.

AIDS in Africa

Unfortunately, the story is very different in Africa. Today, AIDS is a major killer. More than 70 per cent of the adults and 80 per cent of the children with HIV in the world live in Africa. There are eight African countries where at least fifteen per cent of the adults are infected. In Africa, south of the Sahara desert, an estimated 3.8 million adults and children became infected with HIV during the year 2000, bringing the total number of people living there with HIV or AIDS to 25.3 million. Over the same period, millions of Africans infected in earlier years began experiencing ill-health and 2.4 million died of a HIV-related illness. In these countries the virus is spread primarily by sexual intercourse and from the mother to the unborn child across the placenta. The lack of HIV-testing facilities means that most people do not know that they are infected with the virus and so it is spread to sexual partners and children are born with the disease.

AIDS awareness

The governments of many African countries are running major AIDS-awareness campaigns to tell people about safe sex. Uganda has an active programme and has successfully reduced the number of new infections. Education is very important. Research has found that the infection rate among educated individuals, especially women, is much lower. Education is aimed at men too. Now better-educated men are aware of the dangers and their behaviour is changing. However, the AIDS epidemic is threatening education. There is an acute shortage of teachers as a result of deaths from AIDS and there are fewer children attending school. This is because women are having fewer children, either because they are infected with HIV and their lives are shortened or their infected children are dying from AIDS. Many African countries face a triple challenge of colossal proportions: (1) they have to find the resources to supply health care and support to the growing numbers of people with HIV-related illnesses; (2) they have to reduce the number of new infections by financing awareness campaigns; (3) they have to cope with the impact of millions of AIDS deaths on orphans and other survivors, communities and national development.

Future developments

The micro-organisms that cause disease are continually changing. Often this means that previously effective treatments are no longer of use. Medical research has to continue to find new ways of fighting disease.

Genetically engineered defence

The newest methods of preventing and curing **infectious** disease depend on deciphering the genetic code of micro-organisms. Each species and strain of organism has a unique **gene** sequence, which is a bit like a fingerprint. Using this sequence, researchers can detect the presence of a micro-organism and thus diagnose a disease. Gene sequences also help scientists learn how these organisms cause disease.

Genetic engineering enables scientists to alter the genetic make-up of many organisms, from bacteria and viruses to mammals such as sheep and cattle. It is this field of research that seems to promise the most for the development of new disease treatments. There are already a number of **genetically engineered vaccines** including those for **hepatitis** B, **whooping cough**, **tetanus** and **diphtheria**. Genetic engineering allows the vaccines to be made quickly, cheaply, in large quantities, and without the need to use animals.

Eat a banana

Often the health services in the developing world cannot afford to pay for vaccines or the nurses needed to dispense them. Now scientists are researching ways of

In the future, genetically engineered banana plants may mean that vaccinations would simply involve eating a banana chip!

genetically altering plants so that they make vaccines within their fruits. One that is being developed is a genetically modified banana plant. If the research is successful, the amount of vaccine produced in a banana fruit would be sufficient to treat a number of people. The bananas could be dried and the **vaccination** programme would consist of people simply eating a banana chip. This type of development will mean that the plants can be grown where the vaccines are needed, thereby saving thousands of lives in the poorest parts of the world.

Chemical extraction

Plants can be genetically engineered to produce anything from vaccines to plastics, but extracting the chemicals from the plants can be difficult and expensive. However, one way forward may be to make use of a natural process that occurs in plants. During the night, there is less evaporation of water from the plant's leaves and water builds up in the leaves and squeezes out. This is called guttation. Plants that have been engineered to produce a specific protein have been investigated by scientists. The water that has squeezed out of the leaves has been found to contain the protein. In the future, the desired proteins and chemicals may be collected by simply shaking or sucking the leaves.

The drips forming around the leaves of these plants are produced by a process called guttation. If this were a genetically engineered plant, the drips could be rich in a desirable protein.

Engineered mosquitoes

Even more futuristic is the research that is being done on various biting insects such as the mosquito. Scientists are working on ways of getting a genetically engineered mosquito to deliver a tiny dose of vaccine every time it bites a person. If this is successful, the 'engineered' mosquito would enable millions of people living in poor countries who cannot afford vaccines to be vaccinated. The science behind this idea appears very simple, but in reality it will be extremely challenging. Scientists will have to ensure that the mosquito delivers the right amount of vaccine each time, not too little or too much. The release of this genetically engineered mosquito into the wild would also pose a risk as there is a chance that it will breed with the wild mosquito.

Hope for AIDS

It is likely that within 50 years a vaccine made from live, but weakened **HIV** could wipe out **AIDS** in many African countries. But there's a big catch – some people will contract AIDS through the vaccine. Live vaccines are risky and scientists estimate that the HIV vaccine could protect the majority of the population but actually cause infection in between one and ten per cent of people. The vaccine would be most useful in countries where there was a high transmission rate of HIV. Unfortunately, clinical trials of the vaccine would be useless as AIDS may not show up for 20 years and trials only last six to eight months.

Environmental change

At the moment, the Earth is experiencing global warming. This has been caused by an increase in greenhouses gases such as carbon dioxide and methane in the atmosphere. The effects are unpredictable, but it will affect everybody. Some of the more unexpected effects will be the spread of disease.

Diseases on the move

The appearance of **hantavirus** in the USA (see page 43) was most likely due to a sudden environmental change. The freak weather conditions allowed the deer mice to thrive and this resulted in the appearance of the virus. It is likely that sudden shifts in environmental conditions could allow a disease-causing organism to thrive, when before it could not. In Roman times, the climate of Southern Europe was warmer and wetter than today and there were swamps near the coast. Malarial mosquitoes lived in the swamps. As the climate became drier and cooler, the swamps disappeared and so did **malaria**. If the climate warms up again, malarial mosquitoes may move into popular holiday areas such as the Mediterranean and Florida.

During the 1990s, swarms of mosquitoes carried malaria, dengue and yellow fever to new parts of Latin America, Africa and Asia. Malaria is now affecting the highlands of central Africa, while yellow fever has appeared in Ethiopia. Dengue fever is moving north to Costa Rica, Colombia, Mexico and Texas. West Nile fever, also carried by a mosquito, has recently affected New York City and Romania. The initial symptoms are similar to **flu**, followed by a rash that spreads over the body. A few patients may develop complications such as meningitis (see page 29) and inflammation of the pancreas, and older patients may die. This is yet another example of a disease spreading into new areas.

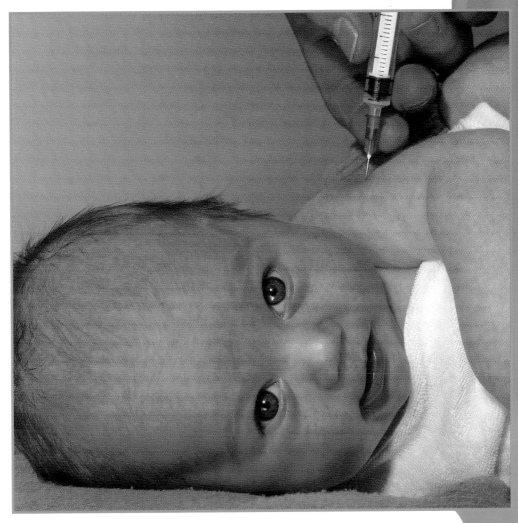

Needles may be an instrument of the past. In the future, doctors may use a 'gene gun'. Microscopic gold beads, covered in the vaccine, could be fired at the skin. The beads would become lodged just under the surface of the skin and the vaccine would be absorbed by the cells.

Concluding thoughts

Over the last 100 years, medical advances and better understanding of disease have led to great increases in life expectancy and quality of life for those fortunate enough to have access to drugs and **vaccines**. But there are challenges ahead. One of the biggest challenges will be new diseases – or old diseases in new forms. Already we are seeing hundreds die from **Ebola** and thousands from **antibiotic**-resistant forms of **tuberculosis** (TB). These new diseases spread quickly, often because they do not respond to traditional treatments.

The limitations of drugs

Previous generations once prayed for life-saving drugs. They are available now, but not for all. Effective anti-TB medicines and treatments reach only a quarter of the world's TB cases. There are an estimated 300 million or more new cases of **malaria** each year. This disease is likely to be a major threat to economic development in many parts of the world. It is now reappearing in areas of the world formerly deemed malaria-free. In a 1999 report the World Health Organization warned of 'a serious risk of uncontrollable resurgence of malaria' in Europe, owing to civil disorder in the Balkans, global warming, increased irrigation (canals are important breeding grounds for mosquitoes) and international travel. In the UK, 1000 new cases of malaria are imported each year from malaria-**endemic** countries. The problem is getting worse due to increasing **resistance** of the **parasite** to the drugs and the lack of a vaccine. However, the application of a few simple precautions could save many lives. Mosquito nets surrounding a bed, for example, are an effective precaution and they cost very little, but only three per cent of Africa's children have them.

Need for funding

It is concerning that since 1970, no new classes of anti-bacterial drugs have been developed to fight **infectious** diseases. On average, research and development of drugs takes ten to 20 years. But there are few new drugs or vaccines in the pipeline. More importantly, funding for research and development into the major infectious killers is totally inadequate. The pharmaceutical industry reports that it costs them a minimum of US$500 million just to bring one drug to market. The combined funding for research and development into acute **respiratory** infections, diarrhoeal diseases, malaria and TB for one year was less than that amount. Increased funding has the potential to save millions of lives.

We need to use our medical resources wisely. More medicines have to be made available to all people, regardless of race, gender or status. At the same time, it is important that some of the most precious drugs, such as antibiotics, be used to treat only those diseases for which they are specifically needed. If we are not careful the increasing appearance of drug resistance may catapult us all back into a world of premature death and chronic illness. Our grandparents lived during an age without antibiotics. So could many of our grandchildren. We have the means to ensure antibiotics remain effective, but we are running out of time.

So, will the world ever be disease-free? The most realistic answer is 'no'. Despite the advances in medical science, we still can't beat some of the bacteria, viruses and parasites that infect us. As soon as scientists work out a way to combat one disease, another appears on the horizon. It will probably be a never-ending battle.

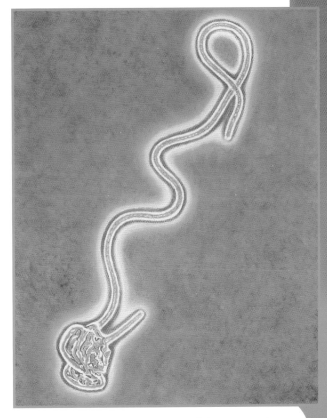

More research is needed into the biology of disease-causing organisms. Scientists know what the Ebola bacterium looks like and how it affects the body, but they don't know where it survives when it's not infecting people.

Timeline

1347 –50	Black Death spreads across Europe, killing more than 25 million people.
1798	Edward Jenner publishes his work on **vaccination**.
1854	**Cholera** epidemic spreads through London. Dr Snow studies the disease and decides that it is spread by drinking contaminated water.
1867	Joseph Lister begins work on antiseptic techniques in surgery.
1877	Edward Manson studies animal carriers of **infectious** diseases.
1882	Robert Koch devises a method using dyes to stain and identify bacteria. He also develops the agar gel-based medium (from seaweed) on which he grows bacteria. He isolates the bacteria associated with anthrax, **tuberculosis** (TB) and cholera.
1884	Edwin Klebs isolates the **diphtheria** bacterium.
1885	Louis Pasteur produces a **vaccine** against rabies.
1898	Martinus Beijerinck discovers viruses.
1910	Paul Ehrlich synthesizes the first antibacterial substance, which is used against **syphilis**.
1918 –20	**Flu** kills 20 million people, a greater death toll than that of World War I.
1928	Alexander Fleming discovers penicillin, a product of the **fungus** *Penicillium notatum*.
1932	Gerhard Domagk discovers a brilliant red dye, known as Prontosil red (a sulphur-based chemical), that cures streptococcal infections and puerperal fever.
1938	British team led by A. J. Evans discovers another sulphur-based drug, called sulfanilamide, that is effective in treating streptococci. It is used to treat Winston Churchill when he gets **pneumonia** at a critical time during World War II.
1938 –41	Harold Walter Florey and Ernst Boris Chain produce penicillin, the first **antibiotic**.

1940	Selman Waksman isolates a fungus that eventually leads to the development of the anti-TB drug streptomycin – a discovery that later gains him a Nobel Prize.
1945	Fleming, Florey and Chain are awarded a Nobel Prize for their work on penicillin.
1948	United Nations set up the World Health Organization (WHO).
1951	Max Theiler is awarded the Nobel Prize for his work on developing a vaccine for yellow fever.
1954	Jonas Salk develops the first vaccine against **polio**. Shortly afterwards Albert Sabin develops a second vaccine for polio.
1980	WHO announce that **smallpox** has been **eradicated**.
1980 –81	First cases of **AIDS** appear in the USA.
1983	Luc Montagnier at the Institut Pasteur in Paris identifies the virus responsible for AIDS, now called **HIV**.
1984	Vaccine against **leprosy** is developed.
1985	Routine screening of blood supplies for HIV begins in the USA.
1987	The AIDS drug zidovudine, also called AZT, is approved for use in the USA.
1992 –93	Undercooked hamburgers cause more than 700 cases of food poisoning and the deaths of four children in western USA. The meat had been contaminated by animal waste containing *E.coli* O157.
1993	**Hantavirus** reappears in the USA.
1995	**Ebola** kills 800 people in central Africa.
1996	Outbreak of *E.coli* O157 food poisoning in Lanarkshire, Scotland, causing 21 deaths.
1999– 2000	UK begins vaccination programme against meningitis C and incidence falls by 75 per cent.
2000	Approximately 3 million people die of AIDS and a further 5.3 million become infected with HIV. More than 36 million people worldwide live with either HIV or AIDS. Total number of people who have died from AIDS since the beginning of the epidemic reaches 22 million.
2001	Pilgrims to the Haj in Mecca become infected with a rare form of meningitis, which they carry back to the UK and other European countries.
	Outbreaks of TB occur among school children in the UK.
	An estimated 3.9 million Americans are infected with **hepatitis** C, which can result in severe liver damage.

Glossary

AIDS (acquired immune deficiency syndrome) condition caused by the HIV virus in which the immune system is severely weakened, leaving the patient vulnerable to diseases such as pneumonia and tuberculosis, from which the patient eventually dies

antibiotic type of drug that kills or inhibits the growth of harmful bacteria. As antibiotics are used more widely, bacteria are becoming resistant to them.

antibody protein made by white blood cells that destroys disease-causing organisms and other foreign substances that invade the body

antigen any foreign substance that, when introduced into the body, stimulates an immune response

chickenpox viral infection spread through direct contact, by coughing, sneezing and touching contaminated clothing, causing a blister-like rash on the surface of the skin

cholera disease that is spread via contaminated foods – such as raw or undercooked seafood – or water contaminated by faeces. Symptoms include diarrhoea, abdominal cramps, nausea, vomiting and severe dehydration. Treated with antibiotics.

culture to grow micro-organisms in or on a special medium in a laboratory

diphtheria infectious bacterial disease that is spread by droplet sprays of an infected person. Children can be immunized against it.

DNA (deoxyribonucleic acid) type of nucleic acid found in the nucleus of a cell, which carries the genetic information

Ebola deadly virus transmitted through direct contact with the blood or bodily fluids of an infected person, unsterilized needles or an infected animal. Symptoms include high fever, headaches, muscle aches, stomach pain, fatigue and diarrhoea. Ultimately, the virus causes all major organs to fail, resulting in death.

endemic describes something that is regularly or only found among a particular group of people or in a certain part of the world

enzyme a protein that enables reactions in the body to occur more readily and at lower temperatures

eradicate to completely destroy, get rid of something

faeces waste material that passes out of the body through the anus

flu (short for 'influenza') viral infection of which there are many types, transmitted through the sneeze or cough of an infected person, person-to-person contact, or contact with objects that an infected person has contaminated with nasal and throat secretions. The symptoms are fever, headache, chills, fatigue, muscle aches and pains, runny nose, sore throat and coughs.

fungi (singular fungus) group of organisms unrelated to plants and animals, which mostly feed on dead organic matter. A few are parasitic. Mushrooms, moulds and yeast are fungi.

gene unit of inheritance that is passed on from parent to offspring. Each gene is made from a length of DNA.

genetically engineered something which has had its genetic material altered by scientists. Usually this is done by introducing a gene from one organism into the DNA of another.

hantavirus viral disease transmitted by exposure to rodent droppings, especially in moist climates, and rodent saliva from bites. Produces flu-like symptoms leading to severe respiratory problems (hantavirus pulmonary syndrome), internal bleeding and possibly death.

hepatitis liver disease caused by a virus. There are three forms of the disease: A is transmitted through ingested or contaminated food or water, B via sexual transmission and use of unclean needles, and C via transfusion of infected blood products.

HIV (human immunodeficiency virus) virus responsible for AIDS. It is transmitted through the exchange of body fluids, primarily semen, blood and blood products.

immune/immunity having protection against a disease due to the presence of specific antibodies in the blood, or as a result of having been vaccinated against a specific disease

immune system the body's natural defence system, which protects it against infection by disease-causing organisms

infectious describes a disease which can be passed from one person to another

jaundice yellowing of the skin due to a build up of bile in the blood and tissues

leprosy bacterial disease that attacks the nerves and causes severe deformities such as loss of fingers

malaria tropical parasitic disease that is transmitted through the bite of the female anopheles mosquito, and if promptly diagnosed and adequately treated, is curable. Symptoms include high fever, severe chills, enlarged spleen, repeated vomiting, anaemia and jaundice.

membrane thin sheet of tissue which covers and separates organs and structures in animals and plants

nucleic acid complex organic compound such as DNA or RNA that makes up the genetic material in a cell

parasite organism that lives off another organism (the host). The parasite, for example a tapeworm, feeds on the host, doing it harm.

placebo 'mock' drug that a patient believes is real. It is given to study the psychological affect that taking a drug can have on physical improvement.

placenta flat sheet of tissue in the uterus (womb) of a pregnant woman, that forms the link between the mother and the unborn child

pneumonia bacterial infection of the lung

polio viral disease transmitted by person-to-person contact. It causes irreversible paralysis, which in more severe cases can lead to death by asphyxiation. The symptoms are generally mild, including low-grade fever, vomiting, stiff neck and back, and pain in the limbs. Can be prevented by immunization.

protozoa group of single-celled organisms

resistance ability of disease-causing organisms to overcome the effects of a drug such as an antibiotic

respiratory to do with the organs used for breathing (especially the lungs)

rubella (also called German measles), a relatively mild disease that causes a rash. However it has a serious effect on unborn children. A pregnant women contracting rubella in the first three months of pregnancy can give birth to a baby with hearing defects or deformities.

septic infected with pus-forming bacteria

serum clear, thin fluid portion of the blood which remains after coagulation. Antibodies and other proteins are found in the serum.

smallpox highly infectious disease. Symptoms include fever followed by a severe rash. Up to 30 per cent of infected people die.

sterilization removal or killing of all micro-organisms on an object or in a material

syphilis contagious bacterial disease spread through sexual contact

tetanus disease caused by a bacterial toxin that affects the nervous system and muscular spasm

toxin poison

tuberculosis (TB) disease caused by a mycobacterium, which is spread by droplet sprays of an infected person or through contaminated milk. It affects the lungs and causes loss of body weight.

typhoid bacterial disease that affects the gut, causing severe diarrhoea and fever

vaccination act of giving someone a vaccine

vaccine substance that contains antigens, either weakened, dead or synthetic, from an infectious organism. The vaccine is used to stimulate an immune response and to give immunity to a disease.

whooping cough (also called pertussis) disease of the respiratory mucus membrane. Can be prevented by childhood immunization.

Sources of information

Further reading

Understanding Disease, J. Ball (C.W. Daniel Co. Ltd, 1990)
World Health and Disease, A. Gray (The Open University Press, 1993)
Man and Microbes: Diseases and Plagues in History and Modern Times,
A. Karlen (Touchstone, 1996)
Fighting Infectious Diseases, Microlife series, Robert Snedden
(Heinemann Library, 2000)

Websites

A number of websites have up-to-date information about disease:
**www.amnh.org/exhibitions/epidemic/ (American Museum of
Natural History)**
**www.sdnhm.org/exhibition/epidemic/ (San Diego Natural
History Museum)**
In 1999 The American Museum of Natural History had an exhibition
called Epidemic! This can now be viewed as an interactive virtual
museum exhibit. There is a related site run by the San Diego Natural
History Museum.
www.cdc.gov (Centers for Disease Control and Prevention)
Factual site covering every aspect of disease control.
**http://hivinsite.ucsf.edu (University of California at San
Francisco)**
There are many sites that provide information about HIV-AIDS. This
one is a good starting point.
www.malaria.org (Malaria Foundation International)
A comprehensive site on malaria: it explains the disease, the mosquito,
treatments and control.
www.virology.net (Virology Net)
A website that brings together all sorts of information about viruses.
www.who.int (World Health Organization)
Features fact sheets on the major diseases and current campaigns.

Author sources

The following materials were used by the author in the writing of
this book:
Micro-organisms and Biotechnology, J. Adds, E. Larkcom and R. Miller
(Nelson, 1998)
Advanced Biology Principles and Applications, C.J. Clegg and D.G. Mackean
(John Murray, 2000)
University of Bath Science 16–19: Micro-organisms and Biotechnology,
J. Taylor (Nelson, 1992)
Advanced Human Biology, J. Vellacott and S. Side (Hodder and
Stoughton, 1998)

Index

Titles in the *Science at the Edge* series:

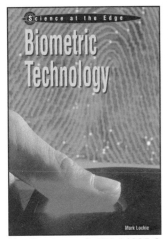

Hardback   0 431 14885 6

Hardback   0 431 14882 1

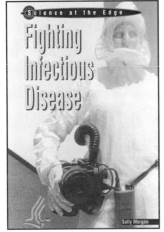

Hardback   0 431 14884 8

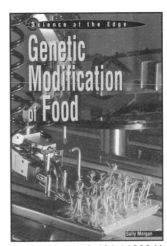

Hardback   0 431 14883 X

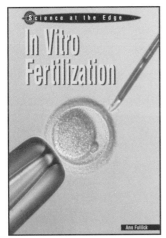

Hardback   0 431 14881 3

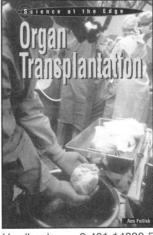

Hardback   0 431 14880 5

Find out about other Heinemann Library titles on our website www.heinemann.co.uk/library